Words $_{by}$ Sam

the perfect soul companion

Samantha Musso

First published in Far North Queensland, 2023 by Bowerbird Publishing

ISBN: 978-0-6457433-7-1 (paperback)
ISBN: 978-0-6457433-8-8 (hardcover)
ISBN: 978-0-6457433-9-5 (ebook)

Words by Sam
Samantha Musso

First edition: 2023

Edited by: Crystal Leonardi, Bowerbird Publishing
Cover Concept & Design by: Crystal Leonardi, Bowerbird Publishing
Interior Design by: Crystal Leonardi, Bowerbird Publishing

Distributed by Bowerbird Publishing
Available in National Library of Australia

Crystal Leonardi, Bowerbird Publishing
Julatten, Queensland, Australia
www.crystalleonardi.com

Dedication

To my children Alyssa, Mia, Tyson and Jazzie;
May you always find your way back home
if you get lost in life.

Introduction

I had endured a lot.

I navigated through my fair share of challenges – the daily juggling act of raising four young kids, including twins. The constant rush, striving to make every dollar count, and being a single parent determined to provide the best for my children.

I realised I needed to step up.

A significant part of my transformation involved healing from past traumas, both from my childhood and adulthood. I took the time to reflect, delve deep within myself, and grow.

Despite a happy childhood and a loving family, my childhood innocence was shattered by the abuse inflicted by a trusted family member, unbeknownst to my devoted parents.

As life began to shift, so did my perspective.
I redefined how I wanted to live my life.

My awakening inspired me to establish my healing business, a source of enduring passion and purpose. I'm committed to helping my clients achieve balance in their lives, all while embracing a vibrant lifestyle with my four children.

I soon discovered that I had been approaching life the hard way. I was manifesting experiences that brought joy but also added pressure and time constraints, without necessarily improving my financial situation.

So, I took a step back, delved even deeper,
and surrendered to the process.

Amazingly, new opportunities, which I had initially doubted, began to appear. These opportunities propelled my life forward,
benefiting both me and my children.

This new approach has given me a clear vision of authenticity. I now enjoy the freedom of more time, financial growth, and a deeper sense of purpose and joy in living authentically.

Like many, I once believed it wouldn't work for me,
or that it was too good to be true.
Such thoughts are illusions created by our fears, limiting our ability to rise above victimhood. It's about seizing life's opportunities and becoming the creator of the life we want, not just what we need.

I am Samantha Musso, and I've fully committed.

I've let go of my fears and chosen to step into the unknown, trusting that I can bridge the gap between this physical life and one of higher vibrations, love, abundance, and financial freedom.

You, too, can have this. It's simpler than you think.

I believe that life is as it's meant to be.
We must consciously choose not to complicate it.

---•—☽◉☾—•---

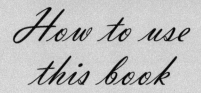

How to use this book

As you flip through the beautifully considered pages of 'Words by Sam,' you will feel energised, peaceful and inspired. Complimented by powerful images, Sam has created a book to compliment life, uplifting the hearts and spirits of every reader.

Igniting consciousness and dampening the illusion of the fears our mind creates to challenge our strength, Samantha Musso's 'Words by Sam' is the perfect life and soul companion.

Testimonials

*"Walking down the hallway of 'The Healing Space'
I felt a sense of peace and serenity. Sam has
created a safe space of such calm and kindness,
permeating the surrounds of the building. I have
worked with Sam for four months and in that time,
she has changed my life. I had been suffering from
the overwhelming grief of loss after the death of my
brother and the suicide of my oldest friend.
My 20-year battle with depression and anxiety
crippled me daily. Sam has helped me to find the
inner strength I needed to overcome my pain and to
help myself live life again.
She literally saved me from myself."*
Anonymous

*"Sam is like no one else in this world, her
selflessness and strength are amazing and truly
humbling. I cannot recommend 'The Healing Space'
enough; Sam will change your life."*
Anonymous

Testimonials

"Sam is exceptionally intuitive and a beautiful human. Her chakra balance is very insightful. Reading back through the notes she received is great. There is no way to remember all of it. I recommend this for anyone who is trying to get to the next level of energy, rebalance and find their direction."
Kevin

"I can't thank Sam enough. After more than 10 years in a lost mind and deep dark hole with no direction, I reached out to her. Her natural loving, positive energy helped me find a new lease on life.
I now have motivation, happiness and a new perspective on life thanks to Sam."
Michael

"Sam is amazing. What she has done for me, and continues to do, is changing my life, one session at a time."
Vicki

---o—❨❫●❪❩—o---

1

We don't grow without boundaries.

2

*Perfect is found within the im-
perfections.*

3

The strength comes when your soul has
genuinely had enough.

4

The ability to sit and be with our thoughts and feelings is only feared because facing our truths means we must accept if we are victims of our lives or ready to become creators. When you choose creator you are open to the flow of love, healing, growth, and true power.

5

Move with love, trust with knowing, be with peace, surrender
with vulnerability.

6

When you lose it all, you have no fear to feel fear; only then does the flow of true surrender happen.

7

Narcissism, manipulation and toxic cycles
can't exist without victimhood.

8

When you start to see all the unconscious
patterns between all relationships that keep
attachment and "need" alive,
you can finally break into true freedom
and love with all those around you.

9

The bumpier life gets ground your
body more to keep your soul on your
true path. When our body, mind and
soul align, we're unshakable.

10

*As your awareness grows,
you see that even the darkness is here
to lift the veil of light.*

11

The struggle between ego and truth will
continue until you learn to trust yourself.

12

Our highest, most authentic self
is challenged during stressful times.
You won't be swayed off your path if you can
quiet your mind enough to listen to it.

13

We may not have the same
experiences, but we all
experience the same feelings.

14

Feel peace in the stillness
of the mind and not fear.

15

Denial is a test from your ego to
see if you can remain stuck.

16

*Actions don't always speak truth;
intentions do.*

17

It's an experience to hurt.
It's a choice to suffer.

18

When the tears no longer fall,
the pain transforms.

19

The actual ending of something doesn't
mean it was a failure;
it means the lesson was learnt,
and it's time to grow again.

20

Unconditional love is free from fear
and free from all attachments.

21

We find ourselves alone when we need
to heal and when we need to grow.

22

True happiness will never come from another.
It will come from within.

23

The root of grief is love,
the heart of fear is love,
the source of anger is love,
the source of envy is love,
the source of resentment is love.

24

You will always find peace when you can
balance the wave of life,
whether ripples or tsunamis.
But first, you must dive to the bottom of
the ocean and come through the pressure.

25

When you let go of all attachments
to all possible outcomes,
a peaceful life will follow.

26

Combine authenticity and unconditional
love, and it's an unbreakable strength.

27

Just because pressure may not appear
to the blind eye,
does not mean it doesn't exist.
It just means the choice has been made
not to break them,
but only transcend them.

The love you give is never wasted.

29

It is our most reactive moment when true growth is presented as, instead, you re-spond.

30

We need darkness to see the light.

31

No one will ever understand what it's like to be 'in your shoes', and they're not supposed to. This is the meaning of empathy and compassion.

32

Everything you can attach to is
replaceable; find those things in life
that aren't, and you find bliss.

33

Our deepest wounds and most painful moments are
our manifestations of the insights of our soul,
in which we can then choose to transcend and
expand our consciousness to create a life that aligns
with our true purpose.
The first step is accepting these as our own.

34

Your ability to manifest the life you want
is far more vital when you align with your
soul's purpose and authentic self.

35

Universal truth is what decides
the balance of life.

36

Truths can be distorted, suppressed,
and manipulated but will ALWAYS show.
When the heart awakens, so does the truth.

37

If you want to live FULLY,
you must FEEL fully.

If you want to CREATE,
you have to LET GO.

38

Only when we 'hold', we are in pain.
When we 'flow', we are free.

39

When you don't know how you will
make it... surrender and trust in the flow.

40

When it's all said and done, the only thing
we have left is our soul; choose wisely.

41

It's the way you handle adverse times
that determines the outcome.

42

Self-love, self-care, and self-comfort will make
you the most potent conscious being.
But it won't come without self-truths,
self-awareness, and self-healing.

43

Once the truth has been revealed,
you get to choose whether you heal
and grow, or suppress and hold.

44

A space where you feel safe is where
all emotions will surface,
and feeling all these emotions allows you to
find safety and trust within yourself;
this creates emotional awareness.

45

Success comes when you say NO
to excuses and YES to always finding a way.

46

Never pass judgment on another whom you
think has everything, as it may be possible
that they have lost everything to get there.

47

To allow and let go at the same
time is the magic of duality in the
illusion of time of both grief and
unconditional love.

48

You'll never have to run when you're the
one who transcends the energy around you.

49

We become 'stuck' when we force, resist, or
manipulate what our self-truths are; when
we accept, let go and surrender to all the
'good' and 'bad' emotions,
we can flow again.

50

The most challenging thing you will ever
feel in life is to feel alone,
and the reason for that is that you are
meant to feel it fully.

51

When you fully feel the deepest of the heaviest
emotions, you'll have no choice but to let go,
and in this moment of surreal ecstasy,
transcendence occurs.

52

It's never the act that creates
your consequence. It's the intention.
Your intentions can never
be hidden from the truth.

53

Love is truly the thing that will carry you
through the transcendence of suffering
and pain; without this, cycles will repeat.

54

When you realise your feelings towards
another are your feelings towards yourself,
your transition can begin from
storyteller to story writer.

55

To reach the depths of unconditional love,
self-acceptance of your truths
must be made.

56

We often run from the discomfort and
pain, which is where our self-truths lay.
The more we run and avoid our self-truths,
the stronger our self-talk in our mind becomes, to the point where we will
no longer be able to run.
Then, you have a choice:
to feel and transform
or to run and stay stuck.

57

Opportunity for growth is on the other side
of that anxiety rush; at the bottom of each
depressive episode, you must choose it.

58

Your intentions create your reality.

59

You can have everything and still not feel whole. You can have nothing and feel complete. It's all a reminder to come back to our centre... love.

60

You want to change your life?
Stop being a victim...own it ALL and become your creator.

61

Trying to process grief in survival mode
will never happen. It's not until the space
is held in which you can feel entirely, in the
absence of thought, that clarity arises. It
brings you back to the centre of it all... love.

62

*Just when the mind thinks it can't go
any deeper, the vision expands.*

63

As the person worth fighting for,
you must never give up on YOU.

64

Pain is a part of life;
embrace it fully and feel what it transforms.

65

You can choose whether you speak your
words from your soul or your wounds.

66

It is our choice whether we wake up
or go back to sleep.

67

The ability to remain open to
feeling whilst in the
numbing of pain will be
one of the greatest strengths
your soul will learn.

68

Using anything external will only amplify
what is trying to heal
internally for your growth.

This awareness alone allows you to become
your own creator.

69

When we allow, we can create.

70

Grief will hold a sense of peace,
while hurt holds anger,
resentment and blame.

71

The love-driven power of speaking your
truth detached from the outcome
is unbreakable.

72

Full surrender to the unknown can be scary,
but it's worth it.

73

To live an authentic life of love
is not about giving another what they want
or need but rather to be in your
authenticity with compassion for those
that come and go along your journey.

74

The hardest thing to lose in this life is YOURSELF.
Once you've done that,
you'll no longer fear losing anything,
and detachment from all will bring
true freedom and pure love.

75

You feel it on the inside before it
happens on the outside.
But can you be quiet enough to feel it?

76

Stability is knowing, trusting, and living
YOUR truth.

77

Loneliness is just an illusion our mind
creates to disconnect us from our hearts.

78

Repressed feelings open our
vulnerability to stress.

79

It doesn't end at the expression of
our feelings; for true transcendence to occur,
surfaces need to be expressed and
'neutralised' into higher frequencies.

80

Denial is a cause for significant
energy locks.
Acceptance is the key to releasing.

81

Ego is triggered in the presence of authenticity.

82

Pressure is meant to be hard to handle;
that's how diamonds are formed.
How we crack under that pressure, though,
is what gives us our unique light.

83

You can silence thought,
remove sight and sound,
cut off touch and what remains ...

you can't ignore.

84

You manifest what you are,
not what you want.

85

Never hold onto anything too tight
in this life,
or you will stop the flow of it.

86

Gaslighting only exists if you have
an unhealed trigger.

Creation brings freedom.

Any addiction keeps you stuck in the
emotional frequency you are
trying to escape.

89

To feel the source of unconditional love
is the most incredible power.

90

Dive through the anger and sadness
into the depths grief
and feel the acceleration.

91

Every judgment of another
is an insight to ourselves.

92

You can allow time to stand still
and move forward at the same time;
you need to see it for the illusion that it is.

93

When we quiet our mind,
we allow our body to feel;
when we feel, we heal;
when we feel, we LIVE.

94

You can't force truth on another
but you can live your own.

95

When you love what you do,
you get to be.

96

We talk about the power of the mind...
But wow, the power of the heart!

97

Your sovereignty creates every
interaction, decision and perception.

98

*Who do you become when
you're no longer 'doing?'*

99

The view from the highest awareness will
show how connected we are, even when
disconnected from ourselves.
Imagine/visualise a single word's
ripple effect and an action's electrical
impulse. Compassion and kindness within
this uniting circuit will
light us up completely.

100

*What you do with your awareness
is your choice to manifest your life.*

101

You can never love too much;
you can, however, attach too much
and knowing the difference
in how they feel is powerful.

102

When you truly feel your emotions,
the mind WILL silence.
It's when you resist feeling
that the mind overpowers.

103

You have two choices
when emotions pull deep;
accept, feel and transcend them,
or, suppress, ignore and repeat them.

104

You will repel what you seek
until you are in alignment
with your true self.

105

Hesitation doesn't exist
when you're in your true self.

106

Just because someone else's pain doesn't
look like yours, doesn't mean it doesn't exist.
Minds create illusions; feelings show truth.

107

Ground yourself
when under pressure
and feel the crystals form.

108

Sometimes,
the hardest part about guiding
someone to their truth is allowing
their actions to match their words,
even if it requires self-destruction.

109

You can give and receive
as much energy as YOU want.

110

Nothing is ever lost.
It's not yet seen.

111

When you wait on anything external
from yourself,
you block LIFE itself!

112

When finding great security from
within yourself,
you becomes FEARLESS.

113

The depths of self-truth will be
the hardest you'll face
until you see they're not.

114

To assume an experience,
whether positive or negative,
is okay for one but not another,
is a judgment made by the ego.

115

Creativity is what makes this world thrive.

116

Envy and jealousy are never reasons
from external sources,
only insight into past heartbreak
triggered by memories that need to heal.

117

You and only you define
all forms of freedom.

118

If you go deep enough, you can become
the transcendent of any space you occupy.

119

*The only purpose of being overwhelmed
is to learn the depth of the present.*

120

Sometimes, we must stand alone
to face our fears and see that we are
never alone.

121

There is no doubt about it.
Your mind WILL create
the reality you live in.

122

We need both
selfishness and selflessness
to exist.

123

If we can self-destruct,
we can self-heal.

124

It doesn't matter what you do in this life.
It's how you do it that matters.

125

Remember a moment of the deepest grief
you've felt ...
now feel the love that sits there.

126

When you can sit and transcend
the emotions of your memories,
your journey begins.

127

You won't heal until you feel.

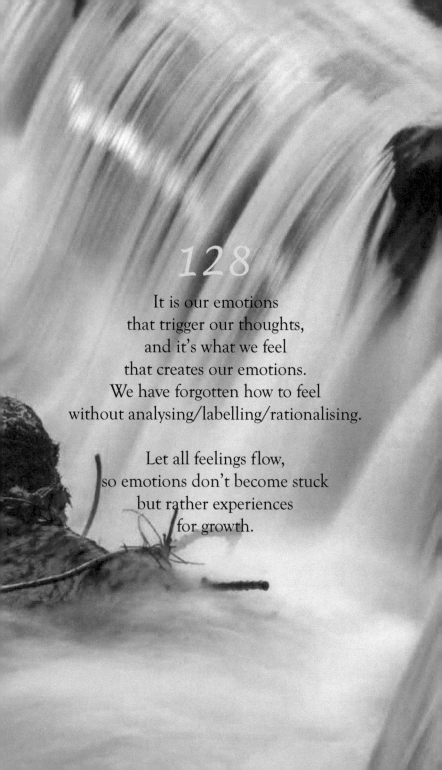

128

It is our emotions
that trigger our thoughts,
and it's what we feel
that creates our emotions.
We have forgotten how to feel
without analysing/labelling/rationalising.

Let all feelings flow,
so emotions don't become stuck
but rather experiences
for growth.

129

You get to choose ...
Run ...
Escape ...
Feel ...

130

It's always easier to avoid feeling the pain,
but when you do,
you live truthfully.

131

The vulnerable ecstasy felt
when grief and deep love transcend
together!

132

Change always comes
exactly when it's meant to.

133

The hard path isn't a change of direction;
it's the path to self-truth.

134

Labels are direction signs to
what needs healing.

135

Anger will NEVER win against LOVE.

136

Balance is easy when you're
in alignment with yourself.

137

The cure for pain is pain.

138

Nothing lasts forever, and all is infinite.

139

To truly see the uniqueness of all
individually, while knowing
the unity of the source.

140

You won't receive from another until you
receive it from yourself first.

141

Love IS for ALL.

142

Empathy and intimacy
are born through conversation.

143

To share all your vulnerabilities with another
opens all depths of your soul.

144

It's not about fighting for what you want,
but the flow that matters.

145

There is no such thing as 'wrong timing'
unless things are forced.

146

As hindsight expands,
so does your awareness.

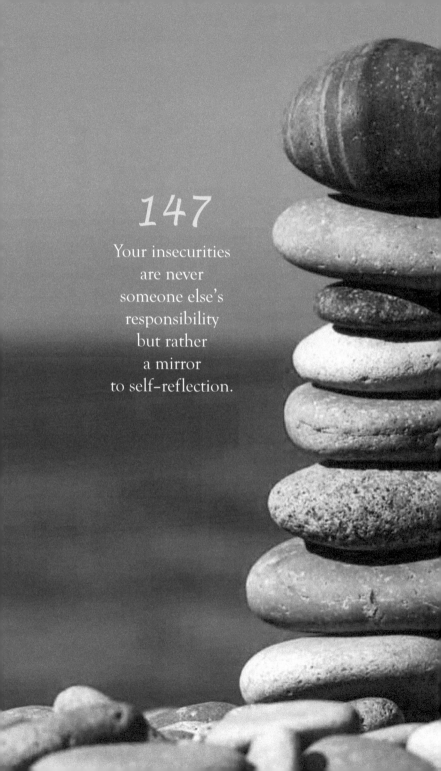

147

Your insecurities
are never
someone else's
responsibility
but rather
a mirror
to self-reflection.

148

Once you truly understand
that you're the one creating
every second of your life,
then the magic can begin.

149

People remember how they feel
when in your presence;
choose your words and actions wisely.

150

The truth may be hard,
but it's always the quickest.

151

Thoughts can be silenced,
but feelings cannot.

152

Doors don't have to be closed
to move forward when your vision is clear.

153

Your biggest chances for self-reflection
and growth will come at your most
vulnerable times.

154

The pleasure in knowing your love
is received allows the cycle to lift higher.

155

The thought of choosing
greater suffering or self-destruction
in the hope of manipulating
a greater outcome
only increases your karmic debt ...
Be the change you want to receive.

156

True victory doesn't come with force.
Force is driven by the mind.

157

The ultimate presence of pure love
uninterrupted by any thought ...
Ecstasy.

158

Magic happens when
feeling, thought, and action align.

159

When you trust the feeling of your path,
there is no need to justify to others
what they think is right.

160

A lot of energy is lost
through fear and anger.

161

Life is meant to be "PLAYED."

162

Every time you doubt whether you're
deserving of happiness
and living the life you want,
you strengthen your ego.

163

The cycle of limitless love is an energy
you can give and receive in absolute ecstasy
if you're open to it.

164

Choose authenticity every time,
and you will never be wrong.

165

There is more than what you think there is.

166

If you don't like your colours
change them!

167

The power of detachment will
leave you connected to all.

168

The ego sees only the ego.

169

Nothing will ever be good enough
for someone else's ego.

170

*Make ripples
and never fear the waves.*

171

Find the play in every challenge
and realise what you are.

172

A truth seeker will guide your words
and actions to alignment.

173

Watch what happens when you live a life
of love compared to a life of fear.

174

You get to choose how fast you accelerate
the transcendence of your emotions.

175

When you lose it all,
you gain everything.

176

Live your present for your present,
not your future.

177

When self truths are no longer feared,
freedom is gained.

178

The longer you stay the same,
the more they seem to change.

179

It will remain toxic
until the pattern transcends.
That change doesn't come from the other,
it comes from you.

180

Unconditional love still has boundaries.

181

Survival mode can also be a beautiful thing,
as it teaches us only to be mindful
of our present.
The difference comes
with the absence of fear.

182

The strength is YOU.

183

It's not that you shouldn't show feelings
of hardship or pain, but rather
accept them as your own
liberating and true growth.

184

Have boundaries, not expectations.

185

You can't release the pain in your heart
or scars in your soul when holding anger.
Loving truly is the only thing
that will set you free.

186

There's a difference between
grieving loss as opposed to
grieving something remembered.

When you've grown up in the dark,
the light can seem hard to handle.

Your location, position
and time are as limited as
your mind thinks
they are.

189

Fear will always be the thing
that holds you back;
until you see that even when
you have nothing, you have everything.
Be fearlessly grounded
and you will become limitless.

190

Judgement has no space
in the frequency of love.

191

Allow your inner child to play
as much as it also needs to heal.

192

You get to choose which road you take,
but they all lead back home.

193

The best way the future can unfold is now.

194

Accepting what the universe is showing you
what you NEED
will lead you to manifest what you WANT.

195

Rebirth is the moment
you break the patterns.

196

The amount of time spent with someone
is how long they need to look in the mirror.

197

Get real,
get deep,
release,
repeat.

198

People who want your light
may not be able to handle the shadow
it casts on their darkness.

199

A free spirit is never meant to be caught.

200

How we handle being hurt
is a guide to our inner child healing.

201

Darkness wouldn't be darkness
without light.

202

Dig deeper,
it's not only the sky that's limitless,
so is that rock you hit
6 feet under the ground.

203

You shine a light on the truth for me,
I'll shine a light on the truth for you.

204

That moment you realise
you've been taken to a whole new level
of strength.

205

It's not that you were in
the wrong relationship ...
No relationship is wrong.
You just weren't ready
to face things about yourself that
the other person showed you at the time.

206

When your body tingles
and you smile at the same time ...
We receive messages
we really needed to hear.

207

Truths don't need explanations;
lies do.

208

When you are in alignment with your
highest self, there is no challenge great
enough to steer you off your true path.

209

It's all about balance …
Peace, love, light,
and get F*#*d!

210

The secret isn't to externalise our emotions,
nor is it to hold them internally …
Allow our energy to move with them
through the authentic truths
that are only love.

211

It is only this moment that is your life.
You decide.

212

Yes, you can feel the ecstasy of love
whenever you want.

213

Can you transcend the intensity
of your patience?

214

To think the greater the suffering you do,
the more good karma will come is only
delusion ... Karma can't be manipulated.

215

The union of consciousness and energy
will start life.

216

Be excited for what happens
when you finally open to the ecstasies of life.

217

To be strong enough to stir
the ego within and return home
upon its death.

218

What happens when your walls come down?

219

Don't dim your light just because
there's darkness in the shadows.

220

When you see and know the journey
for others, but hold space for it to unfold.

221

To wait and move forward at the same time.
The beautiful oneness of duality.

222

You can't separate the waves.

223

The wholeness of love and grief
at the same time.

224

It takes a whole lot of love to love someone
who can't accept love.

225

Become unbusy and see if you can sit
with what you really see.

226

The bewildering.

227

That moment when
you no longer need
to tell your story
because you are now creating it.

We only run from our own shadows.

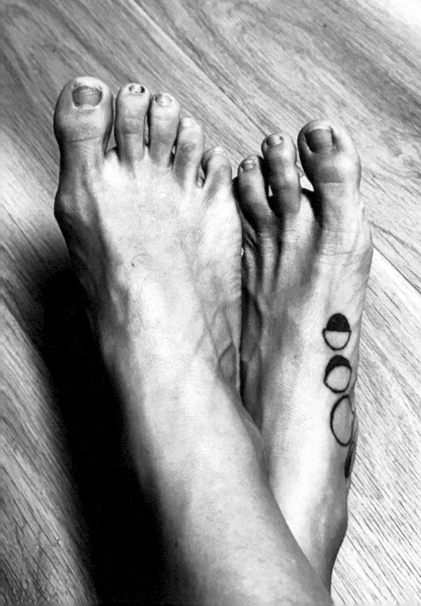

229

Find the beauty in the blades.

230

To keep doing what's easy is different to
a simple life.

231

Selflessness and Oneness.

232

Strength is admirable,
but vulnerability is freeing.

233

The revelation of strength.

234

When you feel like
you've got nothing
to give ... give kindness.

235

We get what we need
until we're able to get what we want.
Then repeat.

236

No matter how we get there ...
get there ...
But the path we choose is up to us.

237

That feeling
when you've sailed through another wave.

238

Deep knowing with detachment to
the outcome.

239

*Accountability for truth holds a very
different energy to that of blame.*

240

Ecstasy ...
the state of unconditional love.

241

Share love.

242

Stop disguising hurt with anger.
Sit with it and let it lift you
unless it's where you choose to stay.

243

Seeking validation from anything external
will keep you off your true path.

244

Hope isn't hope if you give up on it.

245

When you desire to prove to others that
your actions or words are true or right,
ground yourself and sit with the mirror
that faces you, it is this
which humbles us into growth.

246

When the awareness accelerates faster
than the thoughts.

247

Who you were isn't who you are now.

248

It's not about positivity,
it's about authenticity.

249

Find the strength to feel the hurt,
and then you grow.

250

Exploring life with great awareness
gives you greater understanding
and deeper compassion.

251

Love is what sets you free.

252

What you think someone else needs
is really what your own soul is seeking.

253

An insult only insults if the soul
finds some truth.

254

A regret is only a regret if the lesson
wasn't learnt and the behaviour repeated.

255

Sit with the pain,
and transcend through compassion
to be in an ecstasy of love.

256

Every person you meet will always
have something to teach you.
The beauty is becoming aware enough
to see it.

257

Possession is the opposite of love.

258

Patience allows you to create more time.

259

We all grow ...
whether it's in this lifetime or the next ...
We all get there!
Holding hope for those who can't
only lights the path brighter for them now.

260

It is when we resist that we go off balance.

261

Deep connection with a free spirit
is pure ecstasy.

262

Fear of love can not exist,
but fear of attachment can.

263

There is absolutely nothing in this life
we own, possess, or have ...
no person, thing, emotion, money or place.
The only thing we are at our pure core is
love. That is all.

264

Allowing your vulnerability to show
as opposed to hiding it with anger
will heal you faster than anything.

265

Once you have peace in your life,
you will have nothing but joy.

266

Happiness can never be chased
it is only ever found within.

Whenever something hurts you,
you can become wounded or wise.

268

It is our resistance to pain
that allows us to suffer.

269

Love heals ALL.

270

Imagine if every fear you had,
you faced with 'I will handle it,'
every single time!

271

The longer you suppress the emotion
your soul needs you to feel in order to heal
and grow is your own choice of free will.

272

When you feel like you have nothing ...
you have LOVE.

273

What we see in others, we see in ourselves;
let love be life.

274

Polarities, dark and light, duality, together
and apart. Balance is what keeps unity.

275

Sometimes it's not our job to understand
but just to accept.

276

Deep connections with others
amplify with deep connection to self.

277

Growth and change won't happen
without believing.

278

Accept fearless authenticity with only love.

279

The depth of understanding is limitless.
Move with love always.

280

Live with intention behind each breath.

281

You can't take back what you never gave.

282

Accept and release.

283

Nothing is for nothing.

284

Some decisions you make
may hurt your heart but will heal your soul.

285

Allow the goosebumps to take over.

286

Negative energy will age your soul
quicker than life itself.

287

Yes, things can change,
but true soul growth won't happen
because of that new job,
that new relationship,
that new home.
Your life will transform
from the changes made within.
You decide which life you want.

288

The wisdom of an empath will defend those
who suffer greatly because
they, too, feel the pain.
It doesn't mean they accept the behaviour,
but it means they understand without
judgement and hold unconditional love for
them when they can't love themselves.

289

Narcissism will only be hidden
as long as there is someone to control.

290

You have to feel the feeling
and then let it flow,
or you'll stay stuck suffering.

291

We are all pure love at our core
we just need to strip away the layers.

292

The longer you stay a victim,
the longer it takes
for your life to move forward.

293

The constant release of expectation
will bring continued peace.

294

Whenever that light fizzles a little low,
all you have to do is reignite the match,
and that fire for life will burn in you again.

295

Once you accept, there are no excuses,
and you surrender only to acceptance;
you stop resisting the flow of life.

296

Life with a projector will never be easy
unless you are willing to see the truths
they show you about yourself;
then, they can guide you
in your own blissful light.

297

Whatever you need in life will control you;
observe consciously without the need
for anything, and life flows.

298

Complete fatigue will bring
either enormous suffering
or total surrender.

299

To show up despite rain, hail or shine
through the process of surrender
takes ultimate trust.

300

When you have to choose peace over help
... choose peace every time.

301

The perception of loneliness
changes when communication opens
free of judgement.

302

Until you heal your own inner child,
you will continue to see that trauma,
judgement, and experience in every
other situation presented to you.

303

When your purpose is deep and your spirit
strong, the same cycles we repeat are not for
our own growth but for those around us
to learn and grow.

304

Feel it to heal it.

305

Every emotion is meant
to be felt not suppressed,
including love and pain.
Otherwise, we delay our growth.

306

Feel the feeling,
then fly!

Self-destruction is the hardest depth
to come back from.

If the cycle comes around again,
find the answers in even deeper solitude
than the first time.

309

LIFE is in SESSION.

310

The path is always right when things flow.

311

The answers are always in the heart,
the problem is getting out of the mind.

312

You can't connect to anyone else
if you're disconnected from yourself.

313

Surrender all expectations
to find deep peace.

314

Twin flames are truth seekers
who trigger egos.

315

It takes strength to dive deep
but even greater courage to stay there.

316

You will keep facing the same problems
until you heal the underlying truths.
You can never play pretend with the divine.

317

People will always give advice
as long as they're not in your shoes,
and then when they are,
their heart will open.

318

The only way forward
is in and through.

319

Money does make the world go around,
but your intentions of how and why you
earn it will still create your reality.

320

Break the pattern or become the cycle.

321

Self-destruction is karmas inevitable way of
showing that you're not facing
the truths of yourself.

322

It doesn't have to be something right,
it has to be something different
if you want to break the pattern.
But break it!

323

If you want joy, you have to choose it;
if you want love, you have to choose it;
if you want freedom, you have to choose it;
if you want excitement, you have to choose it.
You get to choose the life you want!

324

The blissful peace of unconditional love
won't come without surrender of
full forgiveness.

325

To be completely vulnerable
is to have the full devines trust.

326

The heart knows,
but the mind thinks.

327

We all need love,
the problem is our
resistance to receiving
and accepting it.

Life is a magnetic mirror;
make love your reflection.

329

Love heals,
joy excites,
passion ignites …
now imagine all three.

330

It's not about change ,
it's about coming back home.

331

When the hurt has been so deep,
it will take more than
the superficial to heal.

332

Shed all the triggers,
and be set FREE.

333

Transcend your thoughts,
and you transcend your emotions.

Acknowledgements

To every person along my journey thus far,
you have all shaped the stepping stones in some way
on my journey and I'm grateful for it ALL.

From the Publisher

It has been said that there is no greater gift than to honour your calling. In meeting and working with Samantha Musso to publish 'Words by Sam, ' I have discovered a woman who is not only honouring her calling but using it to guide others.

Producing this insightful and inspiring publication provided me with an abundance of clarity. As the reader, I felt uplifted and provoked by deep thought, allowing me to reflect on possibilities I didn't know existed. It was a truly magical experience to publish 'Words by Sam.'

To those who have the privilege of reading this book and/or encountering Samantha, I applaud you for following your intuition.

Use this book to honour your purpose and discover how to be your most authentic and magical self.

Crystal Leonardi
Bowerbird Publishing
www.crystalleonardi.com

Printed in Australia
Ingram Content Group Australia Pty Ltd
AUHW010955100124
388931AU00001B/1